Filling
the
Pondering
Pool

Haiku by Constance Patrick

Praise for Haiku by Constance Patrick

Constance Patrick's Haikus reflect her years of meditation and keen observation of nature. Expertly crafted, they can transport you to a place you have known but forgot about. They speak to your innermost core of peace. Constance is a wise and generous woman. Her Haikus will touch your heart, bathing it in a well of Love. Enjoy the read!

– Liz Hargrove, Poet, Sedona, AZ

Before I had the opportunity to read Filling the Pondering Pool *by Ms. Patrick, I had no idea that so few words could express such deep emotions, and thoughtful human experiences. This book is such a meaningful introduction to this genre of poetry. I previously read her book Patterns: Poems by Constance Patrick, and I look forward to her future books.*

– Judith Fisher, Retired Service Representative/Trainer, Bell Atlantic, Sedona, AZ

Constance Patrick perfectly captures the essence !of beautiful moments in nature. The juxtaposition of heart-warming sunshine and morning birds talking creates a sense of transience that is beautiful and peaceful. The structure and syllable count are skillfully executed, creating a sense of harmony and balance. This collection of haiku is a vividly thought provoking and beautiful work of art where one can breathe a breath of fresh air and ponder the lasting impressions.

– June Haycraft, Verint, Inc. Product Support Tech Lead, Mesa, AZ

Constance has introduced us to Haiku and some of the best of the teachers of this form of poetry. Then she has written some beautiful poems using this format. The idea of keeping the lines to only three and the syllables to 5-7-5 is amazing. The poems Constance wrote create a feeling of being soft and amazing while still stimulating your mind and senses. I really enjoyed this book.

– Jacque Patrick, Master Docent Phoenix Art Museum, Glendale, AZ

Be prepared to embark on a journey of soulful wonderment and poetic delight. Constance Patrick masterfully captured my attention with her opening dedication and explanation of Haiku. I was enthralled as I turned every page and became captivated by the profound depth yet simplistic beauty of her words, Bravo. I highly recommend Filling the Pondering Pool *on all levels. It will ignite a desire in you for more.*

– Michelle Angela Behr, President University of Metaphysics & University of Sedona, Sedona, AZ

Based on how much I enjoyed Constance's book of poems, Patterns, *I was excited to learn that she has a new book,* Filling the Pondering Pool. *I felt that following* Patterns, *which I feel is exceptional, her next book would be a hard act to follow; however she reenforced my admiration with her latest offering, a very unusual and exceptional book.*

– Richard P. Caldwell D.Min., VP International Metaphysical Ministry, and South Texas Weddings, Victoria, Texas

Constance Patrick is a dedicated poet. She is committed to exploring the versatility of poetic forms and sharing her life experiences with sensitivity and heart.

– Sylvia Somerville, Writer/Editor, Sedona, AZ

I have spent over 50 years in the horticulture industry and Constance Patrick has captured all of the elements of nature in this inspiring collection. Reading her book reminded me why I decided to become a horticulturist. If you take a bit of your time each day to appreciate nature, you will be rewarded with all the wonders that this planet we call home offers. Reading this book will help you to reconnect with earth.

– Gary Cramer, Retired Horticulturist, Cornville, AZ

The laden wagon runs
rumbling and creaking
down the road…
three peonies tremble

– Buson (Translation: Peter Beilenson)

ISBN-13: 9798987120217

Cover photo: IStock

Book design: Naomi C. Rose

Text set in: Times New Roman

Word Crafter Press
WordCrafterPress.com

Dedication

To my family and friends for embracing my creative goals, and for being as excited about my poetry and haiku as I am.

To Michael Dylan Welch a special thank you for granting me permission to quote liberally from his essays on haiku. (See Acknowledgements for more information on Mr. Welch.)

To all things East because I aligned with the East very early in childhood. Thus, haiku wraps around me as comfortably as a kimono.

Table of Contents

About Haiku..............................viii

Ah, yes...Haiku...............................x

About the Kanji.........................xii

Kanji Symbols...........................xiii

Japanese Haiku...........................xv

Rain..1

A Definition of Haiku...................6

Trees..9

Bashō...15

Nature..17

Buson...29

Earth...31

Issa..38

Grace...41

Shiki...50

Becoming a Haiku Poet...............53

Acknowledgments.......................55

About the Poet............................56

Permissions

About Haiku

A haiku is a poem of Japanese origin that suggests perception and awareness about the miracles that surround us in every day living.

It doesn't have to be grammatically correct, for it is but a fragment of nature, making use of space in the same way that Japanese Art does.

Until a few years ago, the haiku was defined as a three-line poem containing seventeen syllables divided into groups of 5–7–5. Today there is much controversy over this pattern. Purists believe that exactly seventeen syllables are required. Modernists believe that the spirit of haiku is the important thing. (Some have written haiku only three words long).

1. All agree that it is a nature poem related to human nature.
2. The season of the year must be indicated by name or implication.
3. It must not rhyme, use alliteration, simile, metaphor or other poetic devices.

The thinking behind this rule is that in so short a poem, poetic devices detract from the thought of the poet in the same way that gesturing toward the moon with a hand that wears a jeweled bracelet takes the attention away from the meaning and symbolism of the moon.

4. It must be untitled as a title imposes the interpretation of the author upon the reader instead of leaving him free to interpret for himself.
5. It must be non-violent.
6. It must be in the present tense. The time is now.

Haiku are not to be read. They are to be re-read. Two examples follow:

Ragpickers searching
something useful on the dump
uncover violets.

On Easter morning
the cicada's outworn shell
cast off for the new.

– *About Haiku*, Truth Mary Fowler

Ah, yes...Haiku

Most likely many of us have read haiku on and off for many decades. We are intrigued by its brevity as well as confounded by its brevity. We also want the brevity to tell us a story, with an occasional twist, or surprise…in only 3 lines.

A tightly crafted haiku is in stark contrast to bigger, longer works such as odes and sonnets yet their succinctness is as delicious as a small sweet grape compared to a big sweet watermelon – and we can savor both. Traditional haiku in English kept strictly to the 5-7-5 syllabic count per line. Japanese count is in language sounds, not English syllables. And many contemporary haiku have no resemblance to the old 5-7-5 pattern yet deliver a more concise moment without the poet's perspective or judgment or emotions.

Some of my haiku are in the old-school 5-7-5 style, and some have been pared down to reflect the brevity of the contemporary style.

Some haiku are mysteriously concise, leaving us begging for more to be revealed. But those are also the ones that leave us searching for more in the world, and ourselves. So we read one. Ponder it. Read it again. Relax with it. Sit with it awhile longer to breathe it in and out mentally, physically…to just "be" with it. We sit with it, let it pour into our senses, our body, our emotions, our memories. We let it resonate in our core. And that's just one little haiku.

Some haiku may be pithy, terse, or humorous, yet their message, in a precise abridged format, leaves us satisfied. We let it in. We let it touch an inner distant horizon. It resonates deep in our core. And we smile as a silent "Ah, yes." or "Love it." anchors a deeper meaning in us.

Sometimes haiku are as profound as Stephen Hawking's understanding of the universe, and as simple as a baby's kiss upon our cheek, or a butterfly resting in the palm of our hand. Haiku are magical – they are as complex as a walnut with a husk, outer hard shell, and two meat halves separated by partitions, and they are as simple as a feather resting on a puddle.

May the haiku in this collection take you on unexpected journeys of complexity and simplicity in a single breath of understanding…and a moment of *Ah, yes*.

– Constance Patrick

About the Kanji

The Haiku Masters were very well versed in both Chinese poetry and language, as well as Japanese. For years, even decades, they studied and became highly skilled in *waka* (poems in Japanese), Chinese poetry, *renga* (a type of Japanese linked-verse poetry), and letters (calligraphy).

Often they chose to write in Chinese for their informative or instructional pieces. Bashō though wanted to give his work the feel and flavor of Japan. To do this he used the simpler Japanese syllabary (*kana*) instead of the Chinese characters (*kanji*).

Over time, Bashō became more aligned with simplicity. Although his poetry grew from Japanese and Chinese classics, he believed it could be simplified, and if understood, it could positively align with reality. In Bashō's hands, haiku was taken from the realm of word games and lifted into a refined level of poetry – haiku's simplicity could present difficulties, emotions, and one's spiritual nature, and at times do so with good humor.

Since the Haiku Masters began their development of poetry from Chinese classics written in the Chinese *kanji* characters, the next pages display many *kanji* characters (not the Japanese *kana*) – several are used to establish a theme in nature for each of the following sections of haiku.

– Constance Patrick

Kanji Symbols

Rain

雨

Happiness, Fortune

欢喜

Nature

自然

Grace

恩

Sun

日

Peace

和平

Earth

土

Courage

勇气

Sky

空

Honor

名誉

Trees

木木

Life

生命

Dream

夢

Kindness

親切

Love

愛

Compassion

同情

Blessed

嬉

Lotus

華

Beauty

美丽

Laughing

笑

Japanese Haiku

The *hokku* – or more properly *haiku* – is a tiny verse-form in which Japanese poets have been working for hundreds of years. Originally it was the first part of the *tanka*, a five-line poem, often written by two people as a literary game: one writing three lines, the other, two lines capping them. Both the *hokku*, or three-line starting verse, became popular as a separate form. As such it is properly called *haiku*, and retains an incredible popularity among all classes of Japanese.

The greatest of *haiku*-writers, and the poet who crystallized the style, was Bashō (1644-1694). In his later years he was a student of Zen Buddhism, and his later poems, which are his best, express the rapturous awareness in that mystical philosophy of the identity of life in all its forms. With this awareness, Bashō immersed himself in even the tiniest things, and with religious fervor and sure craftsmanship converted them into poetry.

It is usually impossible to translate a *haiku* literally and have it remain a poem, or remain in the proper seventeen-syllable form. There are several reasons for this. *Haiku* are full of quotations and allusions which are recognized by literate Japanese but not by us;

and are full of interior double-meanings almost like James Joyce. And the language is used without connecting-words or tenses or pronouns or indications of singular or plural – almost a telegraphic form. Obliviously a translation cannot be at once so allusive and so terse.

In the texture of the poems there is a further difficulty: Japanese is highly polysyllabic. The only way to reproduce such a texture in English is to use Latinized words – normally less sympathetic than the Anglo-Saxon.

One final word: the *haiku* is not expected to be always a complete or even a clear statement. The reader is supposed to add to the words his own association with the imagery, and thus to become a co-creator of his own pleasure in the poem.

– *A Note on Japanese Haiku*, Peter Beilenson

Rain

雨

Sun hides behind clouds

pagodas poke at rain drops

Buddha smiles happy

雨

rain stopped

bees leave kisses

flowers welcome love

Clouds, leaves, flowers, friends

random flaws of time and space –

sweet imperfection

雨

peonies open

softness graces garden

pink faces greet me

from clouds, tears

from heaven

kisses

雨

bare limbs

ecru buds dripping

renewal

clouds drip courage

seedlings release winter

spring drenches earth

雨

hearing birds sing

I stop in swirling runoff –

feet splashing

A Definition of Haiku

Originally a Japanese genre of poetry, now written and adapted in many languages worldwide, traditional haiku in Japanese consists of seventeen sounds (not to be confused with syllables) in a pattern of 5-7-5. Because of differences in language, this rhythm is generally not followed for literary haiku in most languages other than Japanese.

As intuitive and emotional poems, haiku often capture a sense of wonder and wholeness in presenting existence such as it is. Rather than presenting one's emotions, haiku present the cause of one's emotions, thus empowering the reader to have the same intuitive reaction to an experience that the poet had.

Roland Barthes once said that "Haiku has this rather fantasmagorical property: that we always suppose we can write such things easily." A traditional haiku, whether in English or Japanese, has two juxtaposed parts (spread over three horizontal lines in English, but one vertical line in Japanese), a seasonal reference, and focuses on objective sensory imagery. These are the most important aspects of haiku, not merely counting syllables. If a haiku is 5-7-5 syllables in English, that usually violates the form rather than preserving it.

In fact, 5-7-5 is an urban myth for haiku in English, despite how widely it is mistaught that way. This is because what they count in Japanese haiku is not strictly syllables... It's more important to write in one short breath, and to avoid most judgment or analysis... Haiku are ordinary, everyday experiences that give you an emotion based on the presentation of things you can experience through your five senses. Rather than writing about emotions (or ideas), the best haiku are written about what *caused* those emotions.

– *A Definition of Haiku,* and *Haiku in a Nutshell*, Michael Dylan Welch

Trees

木木

lightening bugs weave

strands of summer light

trees dancing

木木

sunshine warms my heart

morning birds talking

trees swaying

buds blush in first light

soft breeze

blesses them

木木

dew reflects sun

buds' flaxen skins

awaken

thin clouds drift on:

moon glows full

black limbs stroke her face

木木

green and white palette

touching heaven

pear trees kiss my eyes

swirling leaves

fall through autumn air

gold curls dream on frost

木木

apple blossoms

new pearls blooming

inhale

sun's day-song calls

joy surrounds, caresses

leaves breathe deeply

木木

leaves free-fall

through crisp smokey air

soundless sleep arrives

Bashō

In a lifetime of consciously perfecting his practice of both Zen and poetry, indeed of making them one seamless practice, Bashō constantly reexamined his aesthetics, elevating the three-line haiku into an art so clearly superior to anything that preceded or followed him that Japanese poets often remark, "Haiku was born and died with Bashō. Only Issa and Buson approach his standards."

The "way of poetry" (*kadō*) of Bashō, the "way of letters" of all kinds, is often said to be more an obstacle than an expression of attainment. And yet poetry is useful in a hundred ways and, despite its Confucian insistence upon the "right words in the right order," is one of the primary paths to enlightenment.

– *The Poetry of Zen*, Sam Hill and J.P. Seaton

The poet strives for the quality called *amari-no-kokoro*, meaning that the heart/soul of the poem must reach far beyond words themselves, leaving an indelible aftertaste.

Insight permits him to perceive a natural poignancy in the beauty of temporal things – *mono-no-aware* – and cultivate its expression into great art. *Aware* originally meant simply emotion initiated by engagement of the senses… the stress in *aware* was always on direct emotional experience rather than on religious understanding. *Aware* never entirely lost its simple interjectional sense of "Ah!"

Bashō spent many years struggling to "learn how to listen as things speak for themselves." [He] sought a poetry that was a natural outgrowth of being Bashō, of living in this world, of making the journey itself one's home. Bashō was struggling to achieve a resonance between the fleeting moment and the eternal, between the instant of awareness and the vast emptiness of Zen.

– *The Essential Bashō*, Sam Hill

Nature

自然

day awakens

morning paints sky

sunrise clothes me

自然

ice-hollows hold steps

recall I stopped, prayed here

birds sang of warm air

red feather drifting

chip-chip, chip-chip pulls me close –

freedom sings to me

自然

warm air swirls

hummingbird stops, glares at me

we share heart beat

air sways the trees

leaves play catch-me in the breeze

earth loves little gifts

自然

morning arrives

sun-sounds make symphony

we are one

sky bright summer
I am lightly wrapped
in dancing warm blues

自然

warm snapping breezes
challenge last sip of nectar
butterfly holds on

pink cotton

spreads over blue vistas

dappled sky hugs me

自然

iris rows stand tall –

royal purple beards wagging

strength…so simple

sun puddles vanish

last light darkens

earth rests

自然

hummingbird flutters

knows flower's sweet gift

soul mates connect

lucky koi

pond safe as sock

two gold feet swimming

自然

evening's gray hush

sweeps warmth from sunset

cold sky births starlight

frigid ponds

fire-hot colors drifting

koi sun-dream…melt ice

自然

small orange flowers

breathe into my sadness

lift pain away

sun-centered cosmos

giving yourself to my heart

sun might be jealous

自然

chrysanthemum spreads

rolls out orange fingers

me, amazed

pine fragrance rides

warm morning breeze

birds sing

自然

longest dark day

sun births daylight

seeds stir from cold beds

petals falling

paint fragrant remembrances

summer ending soon

自然

endings, beginnings

solstice marks arrival

my journey hopeful

Buson

Yosa Buson (1716-1784), an influential artist and poet, is acknowledged as the second Great Haiku Master. Although, in his time, the poetry of Bashō's students and followers had lost a great deal of its force, or energy, Buson referenced Bashō continually as his muse, and for motivation.

Buson's poems (haiku) reflect a painter's observations. He was able not only to capture subtle moments of action and scenes in flow, but also skilled at retrieving nature's unique juxtaposition of images, lines and curvatures, as well as colors and hues, shadows and light.

The artist and poet were so very well matched.

– Constance Patrick

Japanese commentators think of Bashō and Buson as complementary to each other, and call them "the two pillars of haiku." They are certainly poles apart. Bashō was gentle, wise, loving, and mystic; Buson was brilliant and many-sided, not mystic in the least, but intensely clever and alive to impressions of the world around him.

Many of Buson's poems do convey the feeling of the wonder and mystery of nature, but the feeling usually depends so much on overtones that it is likely to be lost in translation. This is true even of haiku that can be translated fairly literally, such as:

The cherry-bloom has gone—
   a temple, in among the trees,
      is what it has become.

Buson always seems to be at least as much interested in the manner as in the matter of his poems. He had an absolute mastery of technique, and an exuberant joy in using it that is a constant delight to the reader. This mastery of technique led him to use tone color and onomatopoeia to an extent far beyond that of any previous haiku poet, and unfortunately this makes some of his best haiku practically untranslatable.

One of his finest – and most untranslatable – haiku is:

The springtime sea:
   all day long up-and-down,
      up-and-down gently.

– *Spring Scene* by Buson; and Excerpt(s)
from *Introduction to Haiku*
Harold Gould Henderson

Earth

土

sun-scented pebbles

new shadow-mountains

dot my path

土

koi glittering

golden silence suspended

beauty centers me

cold seeds

caught in snowflakes' fabric

make landfall

土

time worn street –

asphalt tells new stories

shadows create

breeze plays through boughs

sun shadow-plays on snow

blue jay scolds shadows

土

snowmelt lingers

cloud's stray shadow drifts away

jonquils feel warmth

sun-shadows move –

shapes, structures, gardens tilt

my shadow…flat, tall

土

sun on pine bough

raven's shadow

dances on earth

snow melts

earth warms

feel spring coming

土

snowflakes stopped

from wet leaves, dark shadows

confused cricket sings

brown melting snow

won't wait for spring's new song

runoff rushes time

土

earth grows green

warm sun lifts happy faces

sunflowers smile too

Issa

Considered the third Great Master of Haiku, Kobayashi Issa was truly a more common man than Bashō and Buson. He grew up in a rural area, was burdened with a hateful stepmother; and during further harsh times in his teens was sent away to the city – also burdened with poverty. These early years conditioned Issa to a pessimistic view of life and of his fellow humans. In time, he developed a closeness with small creatures and insects, those life vibrating creatures that seemed frail and weak, and unable to care for their own safety and well-being. It appears Issa saw in them the fragmentary breath of impermanence of life.

Although poverty-stricken most of his life, and suffering the loss of his children in infancy, he strove to make a name for himself in the world of Haiku.

– Constance Patrick

Perhaps the best loved of all the haiku poets is Issa (1762-1826). He was not a prophet like Bashō, nor a brilliant craftsman like Buson; he was just a very human man. But though Bashō himself was loved, his poetry is hard for most of us to understand without deep study;

and Buson, brilliant as he was, had too detached a standpoint to induce affection. Issa, with all his frailties, wrote poetry that "opens his soul to us, therefore we love him."

Issa's unhappiness seems to have been due to philosophical and religious unrest even more than to the actual hardships he endured. He did not have Buson's detachment and could not enter into Bashō's state of complete acceptance. He was not satisfied by the conventional Buddhism of the day; indeed he seems to have been a born rebel against all conventionality.

Issa was a member of the largest Pure Land sects, the Shin, and tried to be a devout one. The boundless love attributed to Amida Buddha coalesced with his own tenderness toward all weak things – children and animals and insects. This was perhaps the best part of him, and in all his poems about them one feels Issa identifies himself with his subject.

Issa's revolt against social conventions of his time was bound to be fruitless and frustrating. He did not at all like the distinctions between high and low and rich and poor, but there was nothing effective he could do about them.

Issa was also a rebel in the haiku world. His poems are – obviously – very different from any haiku that had been written before. In his own time he was actually driven out from his first position as a haiku teacher on account of his unconventionality, and even today there are those who claim that most of his work is not worthy of the name of haiku. Issa apparently felt the contemporary criticism keenly and spent a great deal of time polishing up a few poems that would meet the exacting standards of his critics. These few stick closely to the technical rules of the day but ... seem curiously thin when compared to the poems in which he really expresses his emotions.

Issa sometimes deliberately shifts the direction of an emotion into which the reader has been led. For instance, in one of his poems the first two lines are:

> Snow melts,
> And the village is overflowing—

This certainly starts one on a picture of disaster, which is suddenly—and delightfully—smashed by the last line:

> with children.

– Excerpts from Introduction to Haiku, Harold Gould Henderson

Grace

恩

chanting mantras

blessing bowl spills

healing water flows

恩

black sky surrenders,

cradles stardust –

wonder unending

all the good

within-without, oneness

Buddha's heart sings

恩

soft belly feathers

one leg

heron meditates

chants inflow

fill me

soul touches heaven

恩

mantras

air, water

blessed

sitting with Buddha

and cherry blossoms sweet –

I'm one with nectar

恩

centered

in

my Guru

awake, breathing

standing

morning is hope

恩

in mirror, eyes

reveal calm center –

breath of oneness

sitting with Buddha

soul's sins

released

恩

breathing slowly

behind waterfall's veil

freedom in stillness

storms build snow-walls

karma stuck

I ponder this

恩

universal heartbeat

calls to renew

echoes run deep

lily pad and frog

patient partners –

bug enters karma

恩

earth suspended

in universe –

such magic

Shiki

When Issa died he left no real school behind him, and Buson's followers, lacking his dynamic personality, fell more and more into an artificiality comparable to that which had existed before the advent of Bashō. The revolt against artificiality took place in the closing years of the century, under the banner of Masaoka Shiki (1867-1902).

Japan was at that time still in the throes of change, with the old order everywhere in conflict with the new ideas imported from the West; and Shiki was peculiarly fitted, by both training and temperament, to be a leader in the literary revolution.

Shiki was exceedingly precocious. He began writing when he was about eleven, the year before he graduated to the middle school, and continued to write, in family poetry contests and the like, until he was sixteen, when he left his country school and went to Tokyo. Here he started the study of haiku seriously, and it was not long before he first tried his hand at professional writing… and went on the staff of the newspaper *Nihon*. Here his writings attracted considerable attention, and he had been with the paper less than a year when he startled the haiku world by his famous "Criticism of Bashō." This criticism… is not really an attack on Bashō so much as an expression of youthful intolerance with honoring old things just because they are old.

Shiki, however, was not long satisfied with tearing down. He wished to build up as well and to lay the foundation for a new school of haiku. In this he succeeded, and his advice, most of it given in his newspaper articles, had a very great and salutary influence.

Shiki himself was much influenced by Buson's technique, and several of his poems were obviously inspired by the work of the earlier master. They are not copies, and the differences are often very revealing. For example, Buson had written:

> On the temple bell
> has settled, and is fast asleep,
> a butterfly.

And Shiki has a poem:

> On the temple bell
> has settled, and is glittering,
> a firefly.

The technique is exactly the same the feeling conveyed is completely different.

Shiki died before his powers reached their full maturity, but before he died he and his colleagues had won the battle against artificiality and had brought to haiku a new sense of youth and freshness.

– *Excerpts from Introduction to Haiku*, Harold Gould Henderson

Note:

Shiki's school of haiku was formally acknowledged in 1895. It was known as the *Nihon School*.

– Constance Patrick

Becoming a Haiku Poet

When I first tried writing haiku, my attempts were based on very limited information. The quality and effectiveness was poor as a result. My schoolteachers meant well, but often presented only a superficial and sometimes misguided notion of haiku. If you're new to haiku, you may be in the same situation—without knowing it. While too much information can also impede the poetic impulse, with haiku, as with other genres of poetry, it's worthwhile to move beyond superficialities to gain a more substantial knowledge of the genre. So what is haiku, and how does one become a haiku poet?

The most important characteristic of haiku is how it conveys, through implication and suggestion, a moment of keen perception and perhaps insight into nature or human nature. Haiku does not *state* this insight, however, but implies it. In the last hundred years—in Japanese and English-language haiku—implication has been achieved most successfully through the use of objective imagery. This means you avoid words that interpret what you experience, such as saying something is "beautiful" or "mysterious," and rely on words that objectively convey the facts of what you see, hear, smell, taste, and touch. Instead of writing about your *reactions* to stimuli, in a good haiku you write about those things that *cause*

your reactions. If you remember nothing else about crafting haiku, remember that. If your haiku take advantage of this technique, your readers can experience the same feelings you felt, without your having to explain them.

spring breeze—
the pull of her hand
as we near the pet store

– *Becoming a Haiku Poet*, Michael Dylan Welch

Acknowledgments

Thank you to my beloved Sedona Coyote Poets for their continued support and encouragement. And always, I'm in gratitude to Larry Kane and his photography. He is a master of the portrait, a master capturing performance moments, and a photographic master of life around the world. Check out his website for some spectacular "life as it happens" photos: www.larrykanephotography.com

A special thank you to Michael Dylan Welch for granting permission to quote him liberally on haiku. Michael has been investigating haiku since 1976. He cofounded Haiku North America (HNA) in 1991 and the American Haiku Archives in 1996, the world's largest public haiku archive outside Japan. He founded the Tanka Society of America in 2000, the Seabeck Haiku Getaway in 2008, and National Haiku Writing Month (www.nahaiwrimo.com) in 2010. Michael was keynote speaker for the 2013 Haiku International Association convention in Tokyo. He served as poet laureate of Redmond, Washington from 2013 to 2015. Michael has published his poetry, essays, and reviews in hundreds of journals and anthologies in more than twenty languages. For more information on Michael Dylan Welch, go to his website www.graceguts.com.

About the Poet

Larry Kane

Constance Patrick obtained her B.A. Ed. from Arizona State University. She taught high school English, was right hand for the Drama department, and served as English Department Chair. Her career shifted into business management roles, and after many years of moving around with her job, became certified in Feng Shui and spent several years teaching Feng Shui and consulting in Atlanta, Nashville, and Phoenix. She also wrote several screenplays for TV.

After moving to Sedona, AZ, Constance presented her own poetry with Sedona's Red Earth Theatre in *Kind Art from the Heart*, *Performing Stillness*, *Healing Interconnections: Nature, Spirit, Art*, *Earth Elementals*, *Gratitude Show*, and *Earth Delights*, as well as original pieces presented at the Rumi Tree Art Gallery.

In recent years, she appeared in Shakespeare's *Lysistrata*, and was Stage Manager for *Morely* and *Shakespeare's Midsummer Night's Dream*. Constance has also presented her original monologues with Red Earth Theatre and the Prose and Poetry Project in Sedona.

Her book of poems *Patterns: Poems by Constance Patrick* was published in the Fall of 2022 and is available on Amazon. She also has poems published in *Viral Voices*, *The Stray Branch* (Volumes 26 and 27), and *U.S. 1 Worksheets* (Volumes 66 and 67). Flash Fiction is also one of her strong suits; her Flash (or Sudden) Fiction are published in *The Stray Branch* (Fall/Winter 2022 and forthcoming Fall/Winter 2023). Last Fall her poem *More Umbrellas, Please* was published by The Nature of Cities for their project Shade in LA. For many years Constance has developed short stories around "mountain folk" saying they are her favorite characters, and has presented some of these unique voices with Sedona's Red Earth Theatre venues.

She is an active member of the Sedona Coyote Poets, Western Edge Writers, and U.S.1 Worksheets Poets' Cooperative.

Creating is a remarkable journey — sometimes too big to wrap around but carving it into a Haiku, or imbedding a thimble of truth in a Rondeau or Villanelle is enough to resonate with me and others.

– CP

www.ingramcontent.com/pod-product-compliance
Lightning Source LLC
Chambersburg PA
CBHW060424050426
42449CB00009B/2123